collage+cloth=quilt

· create innovative quilts from photo inspirations ·

JUDI WARREN BLAYDON

C&T PUBLISHING

Publisher: **Amy Marson**

Creative Director: **Gailen Runge**

Acquisitions Editor: **Susanne Woods**

Editor: **Lynn Koolish**

Technical Editor: **Ann Haley**

Copyeditor/Proofreader: **Wordfirm Inc.**

Cover/Book Designer: **Kristen Yenche**

Production Coordinator: **Kirstie L. Pettersen**

Production Editor: **Alice Mace Nakanishi**

Illustrator: **Mary Flynn**

Inspiration photos by **Judi Warren Blaydon**, unless otherwise noted

Quilt and other photography by **Christina Carty-Francis** and **Diane Pedersen** of C&T
Publishing, Inc., unless otherwise noted

Published by C&T Publishing, Inc., P.O. Box 1456, Lafayette, CA 94549

Library of Congress Cataloging-in-Publication Data

Blaydon, Judi Warren.

 Collage+cloth=quilt : create innovative quilts from photo inspirations / Judi Warren
Blaydon.

   p. cm.

 ISBN 978-1-57120-850-7 (soft cover)

 1. Quilting. 2. Collage. 3. Photomontage. I. Title.

 TT835.B51346 2010

  746.46--dc22

 Printed in China

 10 9 8 7 6 5 4 3 2 1

Dedication

One of the exceptional aspects of the quilt world is the commitment of teachers, who in their classes and lectures generously cite and celebrate the outstanding accomplishments of their teaching colleagues and their students. They applaud the achievements of others as models of exemplary craftsmanship or expressive color or dynamic design, while at the same time promoting and showing the quilt as a traditional craft that connects us with past generations *and* a contemporary art that continues to flourish.

Collage+Cloth=Quilt is dedicated to these women, whom I've come to know over the past 29 years, in grateful reminiscence of introspective (and hilarious) late-night conversations in college dormitories with metal bunk beds, as well as in swanky hotels with marble bathrooms. Even though we may only see one another at irregular intervals, we are able to resume a dialogue in the middle of a sentence that began six months before. All of them are intellectually curious and unfailingly honest, and we trust each other enough to wear our hearts on our sleeves. They are women I respect as artists and value as friends and who, from the very beginning, shared their knowledge of quilts with their students and their love of quiltmaking with their colleagues, holding nothing back and always giving their best. The history of quiltmaking as a shared art form thrives because of their generosity of spirit, and we are all beneficiaries of their gift.

Contents

Acknowledgments

Making a quilt is usually a solitary venture—a time when you talk to yourself a lot; a time when you are focused on what is happening (or what you *wish* was happening) on your design wall. You don't hear the doorbell or the phone; you forget to drink the cup of coffee left sitting on the worktable. And you may not eat lunch until 4:00 in the afternoon, when you finally emerge from the studio, still wearing your pajamas.

Writing a book is a lot like making a quilt. You might write a paragraph four different ways and then restore it to the original form, in the same way you audition a paisley print, substitute it with a geometric pattern, and then put the paisley back where it was. You move sentences and paragraphs around, or delete them, the same way you move fabrics from one area of the quilt to another, or remove them, until it feels like everything is in the right place.

But a book is also a collaboration. It involves the interaction of many people, even though yours is the only name on the cover. Without their presence, a book remains an idea written on a sticky note at the bottom of last year's to-do list. You rely on the encouragement of an understanding spouse, the support of trusted friends and colleagues, the expertise of a skilled editor, and the contributions of students.

My husband, Frank, knows what it means to be passionate about your work. His humor, patience, and optimism are constant and unwavering; his hand is my glove.

My grateful thanks to Donna Lamb, of the Schweinfurth Memorial Art Center, who is always receptive to new ideas and who agreed to let me present the Collage+Cloth=Quilts workshop for the first time at Quilting by the Lake. My thanks also go to Kathy Ronsheimer of Point Bonita Getaway.

Cynthia and Jim Corbin, Sylvia Einstein, Nancy Halpern, Mickey Lawler, Jean Ray Laury, Katie Pasquini-Masopust, Ruth McDowell, and Paula Nadelstern were there when I needed their insight and experience. I admire their art, respect their words, and cherish their friendship.

I am very grateful to have been able to work with and learn from the wonderful team of people at C&T Publishing, whose contribution to quiltmaking is truly impressive. They are very good at what they do. They were not only knowledgeable and supportive, but they also listened to all my ideas and answered all my questions thoughtfully. My editor, Lynn Koolish, provided a patient guiding hand and was undeterred by my preference to write this book by chiseling it onto clay tablets. She gently prodded me to move beyond my primitive technological capabilities and remained calm and composed even when I sent her a completely blank disc in the mistaken belief that I had successfully transcribed the entire manuscript with actual words, sentences, and paragraphs. Thank you, Lynn and everyone at C&T—you helped turn an idea into a reality.

Karen Stiehl Osborn, Janet Perkins, Ann Rhode, and Sarah Williams: Thank you for your contributions to the production information on page 94.

The workshop students at Quilting by the Lake and Point Bonita Getaway, whose photographs, collages, and quilts are in this book, also deserve special mention. Their suggestions broadened the range of possibilities; they worked diligently to discover design alternatives and solutions, offered suggestions to each other when asked, and provided encouragement when it was needed. Their enthusiasm exceeded my expectations, and their efforts always inspired me. They were smart and funny, and they were never lazy.

Preface

New ideas often emerge when they're least expected. Some come in a flash; others develop slowly over time. Somewhere over Lake Erie on the way home from judging the Quilts=Art=Quilts show at the Schweinfurth Memorial Art Center, I was leafing through a magazine I had purchased to read on the plane. Attracted by the colors, textures, and patterns of some of the pages, I tore them out and gathered a handful of partial images of landscapes, details of garments, and abstract fragments of architecture. It was intriguing to see them together as a collection of diverse themes, separated from the text they illustrated. When I returned home, I pinned the pages on my studio wall as visual inspiration. They stayed there until, one day, I took them down, spread them out on the worktable, and experimented with different arrangements of randomly chosen portions in different combinations.

The immediacy of seeing potential quilt designs materialize as the result of sliding elements over, under, and around each other to create new contexts and relationships was very satisfying and led me away from my usual compositional symmetry to a rekindled appreciation of asymmetry. Glued in place, the collages went back up on the wall, where they remained, sketches made from paper scraps, while I worked on stitched-paper versions of my Icon series of quilts. Later, I talked about the collage sketches with my friend Katie Pasquini-Masopust, who recommended that the next step in the process should be to work from my own photographs. That conversation at a picnic table on an August afternoon at Quilting by the Lake provided the impetus for my collage-inspired quilts, for a new direction in my quiltmaking, and, ultimately, for my new workshop called Collage+Cloth=Quilt.

Introduction

Collage+Cloth=Quilt is not a math problem. It's three words that describe the sequence of steps in a design process that proceeds from intuition through invention to an original quilt inspired by a collage composition. Rather than making *a collage with* fabric, the objective is *to transform a paper collage into fabric*. The Collage+Cloth=Quilt techniques revealed in this book offer quilt designing possibilities you most likely have never envisioned.

These techniques are presented not with diagrams or patterns to be copied, but rather as examples of a design strategy for inventing original compositions in which you make all the decisions. The techniques describe a process that continues to intrigue me; the quilts that have come from my explorations always surprise me, because, as you will see, they are not like my other quilts. As you explore the process yourself, you will find that the quilt that emerges may not look like any of your previous quilts—but it will look like your collage.

The collage is where it all begins; it's a *paper quilt* that you translate to cloth. Without it, a pile of fabrics might remain just a pile of fabrics. With it, you'll be able to free yourself from predetermined assumptions and constraints, initiate design ideas, reveal a variety of abstract compositional options, and propose solutions for translating your design to cloth using your paper quilt as a design wall on a small scale. The paper quilt is simply another way of sketching and planning a cloth quilt.

Contemporary quiltmakers are often inspired by a favorite piece of fabric or by a quilt they have seen in a book or museum. In fact, much of traditional quiltmaking has incorporated the use of geometric pieced blocks that, in turn, inspired variations on which subsequent quiltmakers put their own unique stamp—either by accident or by intention. That process continues in our own time. As a result, we now have thousands of splendid modifications and permutations of Log Cabin, Jacob's Ladder, Star, and Basket quilts still being made—all echoing something that has been done before.

At other times, a quiltmaker's goal is to make a quilt that is not derivative, a quilt in which he or she assumes sole responsibility for the content as well as for the expression of that content. When quiltmakers aspire to pose their own questions and look to no one but themselves for the answers, revisiting and revising a conventional theme or following the directions of a mass-produced commercial pattern will not satisfy their desire to make a quilt that is not an echo of anything—a quilt that *departs* from tradition, that *adds* to the tradition; a quilt that is not only *artful* but also *your own art!*

Pen sketch for *The Mountain and the Magic: A Color Not Forgotten*

The Mountain and the Magic: A Color Not Forgotten,
68½″ × 86″, Judi Warren Blaydon

Photo by Karen Bowers/Shoot for the Moon

Innovative quilts can emerge from a variety of sources. Ideas can evolve from something as casual as a ballpoint pen sketch drawn beside yesterday's crossword puzzle or as elusive as the image of a dazzling quilt that appears when you least expect it—maybe in the mind's eye or on the bedroom ceiling at 3:45 in the morning.

An alternative strategy is to use the collage process to invent a design composition that will become the inspiration, the diagram, and the map of a quilt that will be all yours. That map will get you started and will lead you to unexpected places and new destinations.

The results may be powerful or subtle, dramatic or lyrical, symmetrical or not, suggestive of a dream world or an imaginary landscape (or not). The process will produce unexpected and imaginative results that will probably be more abstract than pictorial and will certainly present a new direction for you to explore.

Your palette will be a collection of your own photographs, chosen because you are intrigued by their content, colors, patterns, and textures. Your initial sketches will emerge as you play and intuitively manipulate arrangements, combinations, overlays, and fragments of those images—until you arrive at a design that satisfies your personal goals. It has been my experience that you will know it when you see it—just as you knew when you saw early morning light making patches of sunshine in your garden or a pattern of frost crystals on winter windowpanes that these were images too beautiful to be experienced only in the moment, and that you wanted to record them. In family albums, on refrigerator doors, and tucked between pages of sketchbooks are visual diaries that capture memories that can be revisited and that reveal things no one else may have noticed. They are the perfect source of inspiration when you're ready to make a quilt that no one else has made—and that no one else *can* make.

Because every group of photographs will present its own unique set of challenges and will require different solutions, it is helpful to begin by creating two or three experimental collage formats that can be assessed side by side, allowing you to enhance the strengths and diminish the weaknesses of each and to make refinements and revisions quickly and easily. Once you have refined and finalized your collage, you'll enlarge it and begin the fabric selection process. On your design wall, you'll audition fabrics that reflect and express all the visual characteristics of your collage. Then you will proceed to construct a quilt that is certain to introduce new viewpoints and approaches to your repertoire.

The success of your quilt depends on the strength of your collage composition. If the composition is appealing, your quilt will be appealing, even if the final outcome is a modification of the collage. The significance will be in seeing how you respond to creating the collage *and* how eloquently you use fabric to interpret the collage.

Sometimes we forget that there was a time when we didn't know the first thing about making a quilt—when all we had was curiosity, the desire to learn, and the willingness to do the work. So if you're feeling unsure and inexperienced as a collage-maker, consider the words of Brian Andreas, in his book of poems called *Still Mostly True*.

> I have so much to lose, she said,
> if I cross that line.
>
> Like what? I said.
>
> She could not think of anything that day,
> so she said she'd get back to me.
>
> Since then I've been thinking what I
> would lose if I crossed my line.
>
> And I haven't come up with anything either.
>
> There's always another line somewhere.

This book will help you cross that line.

If you are unfamiliar with the collage process, think of it as being as natural and effortless as making marks with a stick in the sand on a beach. Think of it as restful because you can do it sitting down. Think of it as just another way of sketching.

There's always another new process somewhere, and making a collage can be easygoing, rather than stressful and labored. Notice that I did not say "easy," just as sewing your first hand-quilted stitches was not easy. But the same confidence and determination that rewarded you then will reward you now.

It's only scraps of paper, after all.

COLLAGE+cloth=quilt

No 5

COLLAGE: The Map

SCRAPS AND FRAGMENTS: THE COLLAGE IN ART HISTORY

Making a collage involves combining diverse elements and using them in unexpected ways and uncommon contexts. It is a practice that is not limited to contemporary use in the evolution of art. For example, in ancient Japan, poets sometimes included collages on the surfaces of their calligraphy. Cubist and surrealist artists incorporated collage elements in their art. Georges Braque used woodgrain wallpaper glued to his drawings, and Pablo Picasso added a piece of oilcloth to his *Still Life with Chair Caning* painting. Kurt Schwitters and many other early twentieth-century artists used fragments of advertisements, words, letters, restaurant menus, and wine labels, not only as embellishment but also as their primary media. Collage elements have also been present in the work of David Hockney, Robert Motherwell, and Robert Rauschenberg. Conrad Marca-Relli applied layers of painted canvas to his paintings, and Lee Krasner cut her own paintings apart and then reassembled them.

Collage is usually understood to be a process in which one thing is attached to another. In quilt terms, we could suggest that traditional appliqué is actually fabric collage and that fusing one fabric to another certainly is a collage.

Photomontage is a collage in which all the components are photographic and from which a new composition is created by combining elements of several photographic components. Contemporary artists have used photomontage both as a primary objective and as a working prototype that is then transposed to painting, drawing, and printmaking. Technically, photomontage is really what this design process is about, but I like the alliteration of Collage/Cloth/Quilt better.

Collage detail from *Sub Rosa: White Square № 5* (quilt on page 60)

SCRAPS AND FRAGMENTS: ENGLAND AND ITALY INSPIRATIONS

It always fascinates me to see how the different participants in a group quilt challenge use the same fabrics in such diverse ways. When developing this technique, I had hoped that the results would be just as varied if photographs, rather than fabrics, were used for inspiration. I believed that if twenty people were given the same ten photo sources, they would not choose the same five images to work with. And even if they did, they wouldn't select the same elements from those images. And even if they did, they wouldn't arrange and compose them in the same way, because each person's hand moves in an individual way, and each person's eye is attracted to different elements. It's a matter of trusting your instincts; when that happens, remarkable things occur—as demonstrated in the following examples done by workshop students at Quilting by the Lake and at Point Bonita Getaway.

As a preliminary collage experiment, students were each given five photos of England or five photos of Italy.

England

Lynmouth countryside

Trellis in Dunster

Interior of the *Victory* ship, Portsmouth

Building on Tite Street, London

Paving on a Rye street

Italy

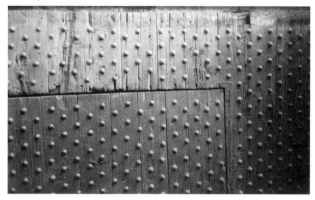

Marostica door

Field of flowers

Fruit market display

Siena Cathedral

Rome apartment building

ONE YOU CONTINUE BRAINS AS THE SHRINK PEOPLE WILL FEEL WITH MINDS OWN TRAPPED THEIR IN THEY ELSE NEED EVER

Type text

Each person was also given one word of type text. Students studied their images briefly, removed the one they found least intriguing, contributed that photo to a group "reject pile," and then added a different photo from the collection, so they each ended up with five images for their exercise. I then asked them to include *some content* from all five sources and use the type scrap—either cut, altered, or in its entirety.

Students based their collage on either a loose interpretation of a classic quilt style or an invented abstract composition. They could cut, tear, combine, layer, overlap, select, and reject areas, and revise their arrangements as needed.

It was not hard for them to cut my photographs apart, simply because they were *mine,* not their own; they had no vested interest, no recollections of a particular locale, and no personal identification with the photos. Admittedly, it does become a bit more subjective when you're working from your own photographs. It's easy to be influenced by memories of events and places, and you don't want to leave anything out; but that would result in a purely pictorial quilt. If, however, you distance yourself from the experience of the place, you can find abstract design elements that can be combined in unexpected arrangements.

I wanted my students to work quickly and spontaneously, to forgo lengthy deliberation, to be unconcerned with perfect craftsmanship, and to view the work as an exploratory sketch. Therefore, I gave them only fifteen minutes to complete the assignment.

As you can see from the results, even though they all worked with the same collections of photo sources, each person's response was instinctive and individual. In addition, even though certain elements were almost always included, they were used in a variety of ways.

England Collages

Those who made the England collages rearranged the row of red bowling game balls in several different ways.

Fay Martin combined trellises, textural paving stones, and architecture in unexpected size relationships, nestling a red globe between the gables.

Christine Milton rearranged the globes and clustered the ship's interior elements.

Barbara Shuff Feinstein rearranged the red globes into an arc and tilted the pictorial elements at dizzying angles.

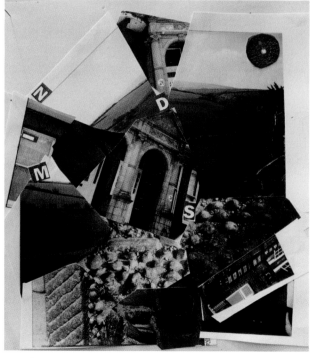

Jennifer Bigelow created an imaginary world with foreground, middle distance, and horizon, using a variety of scale and one red sun.

Sharona Fischrup anchored the corners and center of her design with the wooden balls. The Lynmouth landscape frames the trellis—airy and atmospheric above, dark and shadowy beneath.

Joanne Wietgrefe suggested a recessed doorway or alcove, outlined at one edge with red globes.

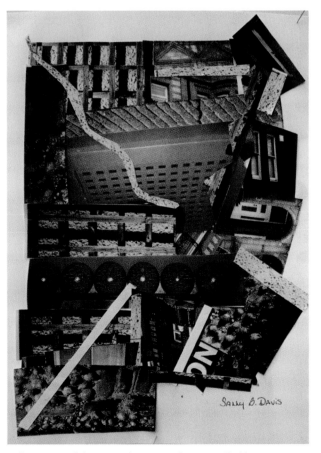

Sally B. Davis did a more abstract and crazy-quilt–like composition.

In a double-exposure view, Claudia Alldredge jux-taposed an expanse of countryside landscape with urban buildings vying for space.

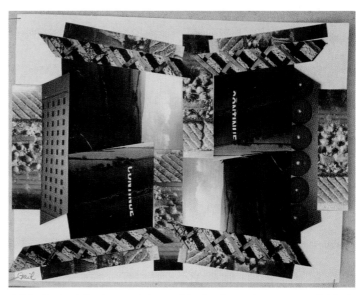

Gail Retka Angiulo clustered views of the landscape in a Four-Patch block variation, alternating and spinning them in a clockwise rotation.

Serene and balanced, the left-right symmetry of Ann Rhode's collage, as well as the projecting element at the bottom, suggest we could magically walk into the landscape.

You'll notice that the color intensity in the collages of Gail, Ann, and Sharona is different from the other England examples. This occurred when I was preparing the photos for class. Even though my printer was warning me that the cartridge ink was low, I continued printing.

Italy Collages

In the Italy collages, a cathedral arch in Siena was an appealing element.

Carole Burton sliced and arranged architectural elements to create a many-layered collage.

Janet Ozard Root combined natural and architectural elements and only a small fragment of the arch.

Peggy Montesano used the arch as a center panel and surrounded it with darker values and vivid colors.

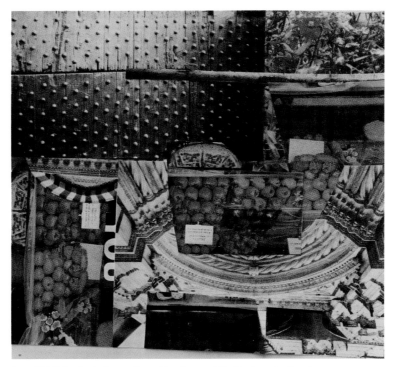

Jean Biddick alluded to a distant horizon, while the inverted arch suggests a vessel holding the fruit.

Emily Shuff Klainberg let the buildings rise to the sky and placed the highest floor of the Rome apartment at the top of what seem to be archaeological layers.

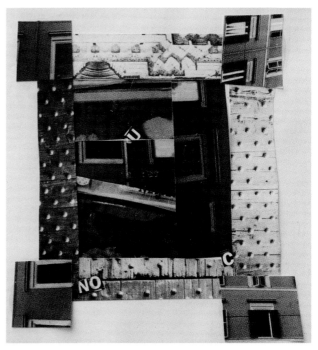

Mary C. Lowe paid homage to a traditional quilt block by using corner squares from the Rome apartment and not including the arch at all.

In Florence Barnhart's square with borders and corner squares version, the field of wildflowers takes center stage, bordered by contrasting architectural details.

This exercise gave students a chance to do a practice collage before cutting up their own photos. It also established the idea that collage doesn't have to be intimidating. Finally, it proved that a collage tells us more about the potential qualities of a design than a pencil sketch does; thus it is a more concrete starting point because it gives more information, more quickly.

These examples show that your collage can be a quick way to assess color, value contrasts, texture, scale, content, composition, and the degree of interest in going further. Seeing the collage allows you to make revisions and adjustments before progressing to the design wall.

Deanna M. Davis isolated a vertical sliver of the Rome apartment building and created a tower, soaring upward, framed by a mixture of natural and architectural elements.

THE APPEAL OF COLLAGE

I have always been in awe of quiltmakers who can intuitively gather fifteen fabrics after breakfast and have a gorgeous quilt sewn together before dinner, without overthinking whether to substitute a turquoise paisley with a blue-violet stripe. I admire their capacity to react spontaneously to what is on their design wall, to pin up large pieces of favorite fabrics and take them down, trying others and experimenting until they find an expressive combination. I have never been very successful at randomly choosing yardage from my fabric shelves, putting it on my design wall, and waiting for it to tell me what to put beside it; usually I wait to see if it falls off. I think I have an inherent dread of making a hasty decision to cut a two-yard piece of hand-painted silk into six-inch squares and then wishing I had left it intact. So for me, the collage process has introduced a work method that solves the problem of chronic indecisiveness.

The following three quilts are typical examples of my quilts before collage. These, like most of my previous quilts, involve symmetry to the left and right of a center vertical. Most of my pre-collage quilts began with an idea that I wanted to express or a memory that I wanted to record. They were about content first, and that content directed my initial fabric choices and also inspired the compositions. That instinctive left-right symmetry seemed to come naturally; I felt satisfied with the restful and calming aspects it provided, and it never occurred to me to abandon that in favor of something more adventurous and daring.

The Mountain and the Meadow: Field of Dreams, Judi Warren Blaydon, 55½" × 70"

This quilt incorporates influences of landscapes, crazy quilts, and temple altars. Mt. Fuji, rising above the horizon, is obscured by passing clouds and reappears again. The clouds are defined in the quilted lines as well as in the pieced construction. The strip-pieced meadow was done with floral and foliage prints. Machine pieced, hand quilted, and beaded.

Photo by Mark Kurczewski/MARK PACKO Filmwerks Studios

Icon: Saint Gertrude / Patron Saint of Gardeners, Judi Warren Blaydon, 23½" × 19½"

A fictional St. Gertrude is enshrined in a three-dimensional environment of blossoms, sky, botanical references, a glass vial of flower seeds, and flower labels. Inkjet-printed collage elements are used as embellishment. From a series of machine-pieced, hand-quilted, and beaded standing altars.

A Room with a View: Seasons Pass, Judi Warren Blaydon, 33½" × 23½", from the collection of Ann Rhode

This quilt commemorates the passage of time, the ending of winter, and the coming of spring. In a simultaneous view of the seasons, snow falling outside the window is contrasted with a forecast of sunlight and the arrival of new foliage. Machine pieced, hand quilted, and beaded.

Unlike the two Icon quilts and *Field of Dreams* (previous page), which were inspired by content and theme, the quilts in my ongoing Sub Rosa series (this page) begin with a photo-collage "sketch" that introduces an asymmetrical compositional mode that I had never used before. The next examples are shown to demonstrate how the departure from my usual work method enabled me to shift from a comfortable symmetrical style into a less predictable format, which then allowed me to see and think in new ways. The same thing can happen for you as you explore the process.

Although the Sub Rosa quilts are more abstract than pictorial, the compositions are suggestive of landscape, and the visual content of the fabrics reflects natural elements—botanical imagery, textures, and banks of clouds. Establishing a horizon line at an unexpected level (either very high or very low in the composition) allows me to suggest terrain, panoramic skies, or distant vistas of imaginary worlds.

Sub Rosa: Last Light, Judi Warren Blaydon, 40″ × 34″

Sub Rosa: Curtain, Judi Warren Blaydon, 63″ × 52″

MAKING EXPERIMENTAL COLLAGES

Supplies

- Photographs
- Clear removable tape
- 8½″ × 11″ white paper
- Paper scissors, rotary cutter, and cutting mat
- Rubber cement or gluestick
- Quilter's Design Mirrors (see Resources, page 94) or 2 small straight-edged mirrors
- Prismacolor Premier or Scholar color pencils (box of 12 colors)
- White drawing pencil and ebony pencil (available at art supply stores)
- Pencil sharpener
- *Optional:* Some lines of newspaper/magazine text type, chosen for style *and* content

Photographs

You can use prints from either film or digital cameras. Use whichever type of camera you are most comfortable with. To begin your journey into collage, the first thing you need is a collection of images from which to draw inspiration. Your collage elements will come from photographs you have taken, selected because you love looking at them and because you love seeing them together. The content may or may not be thematically related; instead, look for compelling colors, details of random and formal patterning, subtle and dramatic value contrasts, graphic design, manufactured and natural imagery—in other words, things that catch your eye.

Imagine yourself walking past bolts of cloth in the fabric store. Think about the certainty with which you grab a bolt of cloth, saying, "I really love this!" Now, replace the idea of those fabric shelves with piles of photographs; you can make the same confident choices. Trust your instincts. Gather your photos with the same bravura that you gather bolts of fabric before you take them to the cutting counter at the fabric store.

Make your final choices of photos by determining which images you love most. In your collage, you'll be combining fragments of several varied sources, though sometimes you might work from a single complex image.

Don't base your selections on whether or not you already have yardage in your fabric collection that will express that specific visual content. I have found that when I respond to the visual content of a particular photograph, I often already have fabrics that reflect some of those same qualities, because the same instincts are at work.

Your quilt will only be as intriguing as your collage, and your collage will only be as intriguing as the scraps, details, and fragments from your photographs. If you love your photo swatches, you will love your collage. If you love your collage, you will love your quilt! It's all about believing in your collage and letting that collage inspire a quilt.

The quilt that emerges will be more abstract than pictorial. But that *does not* mean you shouldn't consider including in your preliminary choices your favorite photo of a sunset at the Grand Canyon or the photo of the Chrysler building that you took while lying on your back in the street and looking up. It *does* mean that while you may use details of the Chrysler building or a forest in Italy, you will not be making a picture quilt. It also means that although your quilt may include pictorial references and symbols, these will be present in combination with geometric pieced elements or will be used cropped, reduced, or enlarged to complement and contrast with abstract areas within the composition.

Gathering Photographs

First, make a random gathering of your favorite *existing photographs*. This collection might (or might not) be thematically related. It might include a landscape, a close-up of the upholstery on your grandma's sofa, the glaze on your favorite ceramic bowl, an artfully composed collection from a very special trip, or even a group of photos of your own quilts! As long as you like them individually and together, put them in the "maybe" pile.

Then increase your options and widen your horizons by generating *new photographs*. Point your camera as though each photograph will magically become fabulous fabric. Take an expansive general view, and then zoom in to record more definitive details and close-ups. In these new photos, you may discover subtle components that occur in the transition from three-dimensional reality to two-dimensional photograph that you didn't notice even as you clicked the shutter. Whether you choose to include these nuances or not, it's all a good exercise in looking.

GETTING STARTED

Don't be limited by the following ideas; instead, use them to help you focus and to suggest your own additions to the lists of ideas. The following are some themes and subjects to consider as you look for details, close-ups, abstract views, colors, textures, and patterns. Whether you're using previously taken or new photographs, you can keep this part of your search uncomplicated and quick simply by choosing:

- Something botanical
- Something mechanical
- A texture
- A pattern
- A landscape

Or you can be more thoughtful and thorough in your investigation of specific possibilities.

Architectural and Mechanical Details

Linear patterns in a pile of metal sidewalk grills in London's Chelsea district

Don't look just for postcard views. Find some unusual vantage points when recording both classic and contemporary landmarks and urban or rural buildings. Don't focus on just the wonderful historical buildings, the significant architectural example, or your cottage at the lake; rather, look at *all the little details.*

- Hardware
- Doorknobs and hinges
- Peeling paint
- Embellishments
- Decorative textures
- Neon signs
- Manhole covers
- Cornices and pediments
- Grills, fences, and gates
- Graffiti
- Trellises and gazebos
- Graphics on buildings
- Electric meters
- Overhead wires
- Billboards

Look slowly to really see:

- Not just the cathedral in Siena but also the details of the black-and-white surface patterns
- Not just the antique Jaguar, but also the grill, the hubcap, or the dashboard

Now, write down your own ideas.

Interior Environments

A view of my kitchen window

The interior of your home is already full of your favorite things. Things you treasure and display, arrange and rearrange (and hopefully, occasionally dust). They express *you*.

- Shadows cast from sunlit windows

- Dining room chandeliers

- Antique silverware or jewelry

- Upholstery fabric patterns and textures

- Collections of napkin rings or teapots or hats or vintage shoes

- The inside of your piano or your pantry or your spice cupboard

- The contents of your refrigerator's vegetable drawer

- A still life of strainers, potato mashers, tongs, kitchen utensils, and appliances

- Embroidery on pillowcases, lace tablecloths, and curtains

- The labyrinth of wires behind your computer desk

Look slowly to really see:

- Not just the vintage dress in your closet, but also the ruffles or the smocking or the buttons on the dress

- Not just the belt, but also the buckle

Now, write down your own ideas.

Nature

Let geographic locales, terrains, and seasons inspire you.

A snowfall turns the backyard into a stage set for an Ice Follies movie.

Look for sweeping vistas as well as close-up views:

- Not just the coastline terrain, but also the seashells, sea glass, and stones

- Not just the tree, but also the texture of the bark, the pattern of leaves, the network of branches, the maze of twigs

- Not just the garden, but also the blossoms, individual petals, stems, and thorns

- Not just the meadow, but also the grasses

- Not just the field of Queen Anne's Lace, but also the details of the blossoms

- Not just the ocean, but also the kelp, the pebbles, the foam, the colors of the water, the stones under the surface

- Not just the desert, but also the wind patterns on the sand and the needles on the cactus plants

- Not just the sky, but also its changing colors

- Not just the cloud formations, but also the rain and snow, both falling and fallen

Now, write down your own ideas.

SELECTING AND PREPARING YOUR PHOTOS

Gathering a representative collection of photos might seem like an insurmountable task, especially in an era when digital cameras allow us to generate, file, and print hundreds of outstanding choices. Your job is to browse and gather an assortment of your previously taken photographs, as well as new photos. As you begin the selection process, try to assemble images you wish were available in cloth yardage. Again, don't make your final choices because you already have the ideal fabric; choose them because they are gorgeous photos.

Looking for Content

Subject matter can originate from nature and landscapes, urban architecture and historic buildings, industrial and functional objects—from garbage can lids to insects. On the following pages are examples of photographs contained in some of the collages that inspired quilts you'll find in a later chapter. They demonstrate a broad and varied collection of subjects and themes. Notice the color and value contrasts, as well as the textures, patterns, and variety of scale.

Jean Biddick found inspirations in architecture in Kentucky, Massachusetts, and New York, and in a Mexican bird of paradise. Her collage and quilt are on pages 70–71.

Photos by Jean Biddick

In the collage and quilt on pages 74–75, flowers, fruit, foliage, and a Luna moth inspired **Mary C. Lowe**.

Photos by Mary C. Lowe

Janet Ozard Root used photos of utilitarian and decorative objects, such as garbage can lids, tires, car headlights, and decorative wrought iron, to inspire her collage and quilt on pages 66–67.

Photos by Janet Ozard Root

Choosing Your Photos

Spread out your collection of photos on a table, or pin them to a work wall. First, choose three that are your favorites, both individually and together. These do not have to be thematically related (several gray beach pebble images might not be very interesting anyway). Make these initial selections based on their visual appeal and because you love everything about them.

Set aside some photos that don't seem promising, but don't reject them; just remove them from contention for now. Then, from the remaining choices, pick three more that complement and contrast with your first group.

You now have a core group of six photos, portions of which will be the major elements for your collage. If you want to increase your creative options by including a few more images, ten or eleven photo sources would be more than ample; twenty would definitely be too many!

Use a color copier or printer to make two or three color-accurate, actual-size copies of each of your first choice photos.

Then generate different sizes of each photo to add visual interest and variety of scale to your collage. Reduce each photo so it is 50–75% of the original size, and then enlarge each photo to about 125%. Make two copies of each new size.

When you're copying, combine originals whenever possible, and keep the original photos handy in case you need to print additional copies.

tip

Even sophisticated copiers and printers sometimes produce uninvited color changes. Try to achieve precise color reproduction. If your copies are too cool, too warm, or too intense and not as accurate as you would like, reference the original photograph for color information, and use the copies for design planning. It may even turn out that you like the altered colors better.

MAKING A VIEWING WINDOW

Before you begin, make a viewing window so you can visually isolate and zoom in on details to discover unconventional views within your photographs.

A viewing window works best when it is made of two separate right, or L, angles that can be shifted and moved to make the view larger or smaller or changed from a square to a rectangle. A hole cut in a single piece of paper does not offer that flexibility. Instead, make your L angles from something sturdy, such as heavy white paper or poster board.

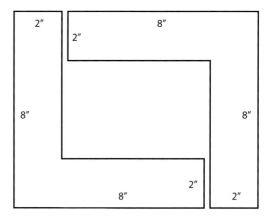

I like these dimensions for viewing windows because they are wide enough to momentarily hide the parts of the image that are in the periphery, allowing me to focus on one specific area at a time.

Using Your Viewing Window

Viewing angles placed over an interior of the Palazzo Vecchio in Florence, Italy

When you've made your viewer, try the following experiment: Use the viewing window to isolate a small square area of an asymmetrical abstract view within this photograph (above) of a bridge near the New Tate Gallery in London.

Now, find two more! Imagine them enlarged.

Try mirroring one of the images by using two small, straight-edged mirrors.

To draw mirror images, and to make copies of a particular element that you've used up in your collages, use your colored pencils. Use them forcefully, rather than hesitantly, to make the colors as strong as those in the collage element.

If the color in your photo is very vivid (left), don't be timid with the pencils (center). Duplicate the color intensity as closely as you can (right).

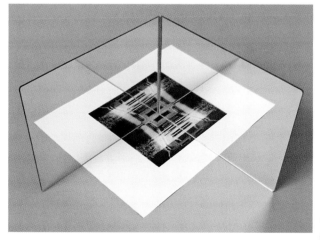

Use mirrors to see alternate views of design elements.

COLLAGE FORMATS

The following nine photographs were used in the collages on pages 34–36, 60, and 90.

Japan

Incense fire, Asakusa Temple, Tokyo

Display window at Wako Department Store, Ginza, Tokyo

Interior views, Todai-ji Temple, Nara

Mexico City, Mexico

Wood wall with painted numbers

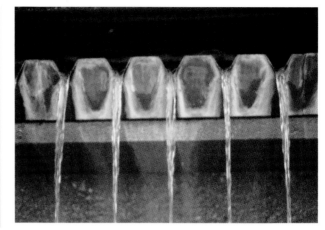

Fountain waterfall

Aix-en-Provence, France

Wall with graffiti

The following collages—using these photos from Japan, Mexico, and France—show a variety of recognizable quilt styles. Even the best-loved, most easily recognized classic blocks take on special qualities when the fabrics express the personal memories from the photographs you use to make your collage. No matter where your current quiltmaking interest lies, you'll find examples to get you started.

Chairs outside a cafe

Rock concert posters

Traditional Quilt Formats

Center medallion

Crazy quilt

Stripy

In this variation of the crazy quilt collage, a small section was isolated and rotated to create another design possibility.

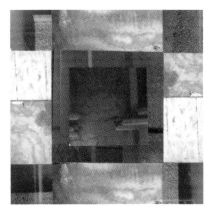

The following interpretations, based on squares with borders and corner squares, reflect diverse responses to the same collage inspiration.

Square within a square with borders and corner squares

Made by Joanne Wietgrefe

Made by Jean Biddick

Made by Janet Ozard Root

Square within a square within a square

As a warm-up exercise, try some of the preceding formats using color copies of your own photographs. Which traditional formats would you add to the list?

New Growth, Peggy Montesano, 38½″ × 39½″

New Growth is a square with borders and corner squares that was inspired by a different group of photographs. Peggy appliquéd a magnified view of botanical content in the center, surrounded it with misty foliage, and bordered it asymmetrically with fluted columns.

Innovative Quilt Formats

When collage elements are arranged in nonsymmetrical formats, they create abstract pieced compositions that suggest enigmatic, nonpictorial environments.

Stif/1 is an asymmetrical arrangement of disconnected floating elements.

Rock demonstrates not limiting yourself to placing collage pieces edge to edge. Float some elements on a background, and slip some under and over others to create transparencies and shapes that align to create a larger element.

Stif/2 is an isolated square from the interior of *Stif/1*, with other elements added to suggest transparent and opaque layers.

tip

To make your designs more dynamic, watch out for *puzzle pieces*—pieces that are placed edge to edge. Replace these puzzle pieces by layering images in front of and behind other elements, creating the potential for *transparency*—when one shape crosses another and creates another new element.

Image-on-Image Manipulations

Designs that employ pictorial content can be used to create surprising, invented, imaginary environments. Rather than using a photograph in its entirety, as you might to inspire a pictorial quilt, take apart one photo and reassemble it in a new way—perhaps pairing it with another photo of a similar subject or with something entirely different.

If your final collage includes recognizable pictorial information or amorphous shapes, you'll be able to create those areas in fabric using either traditional or fused appliqué processes. In this way, even small details like the feathery edges of foliage can be accomplished.

Two photographs taken in Tuscany, Italy

Contrast of Scale

Create an unlikely environment by combining an enlarged portion of a single photograph within the original or by superimposing a reduced image of that same portion.

Contrast of scale creates double trees.

A photograph of pavement textures in Florence, Italy, is seen with one enlarged detail superimposed in the center, creating a square within a square.

Contrast of scale changes a Rome apartment building into abstract architecture.

In this example, the Florence pavement photos are used three times, manipulated in three different scales, to create a more complex result. Although lacking dramatic color and value contrasts, the pavement images emphasize texture and changes of scale.

Common Theme

Create a common theme using images taken from different photo sources. In this example, elements from both photographs of trees in Italy were combined in two different scales. You could also superimpose a reduced element from one photo on an enlarged element from another photo. As you explore this method, experiment with different degrees of change in scale.

Combined Tuscan forests

Contrast of Content and Scale

Create a fanciful world in which visual irony places two dissimilar subjects in a whimsical and unlikely pairing. Rather than copying a single photo in fabric to make a pictorial quilt, the goal is to combine two unrelated pictorial themes to create an environment that doesn't exist—for instance, a comet in your kitchen or a vase of flowers atop the Empire State Building. You might also look for photos that remind you of insider family jokes.

Rome apartment within the forest

The forest on the facade of the apartment

Options for Complex Photos

Light and shadow on a canal in Venice

Some photographs are complex enough and rich enough in detail, color, texture, and contrast of value and content that they offer several pictorial elements that become abstract when you conceal the rest of the image. These complex photographs will have more than just one potential composition; use your viewer to isolate and audition them.

View A   View B   View C

Three potential compositions found within the Venice canal photo

A more expanded translation of View C brings more details to the motif.

Two variations using the expanded View C, in which a series of slivers that diminish in size are positioned to move in steps, outward from the side edges. They begin with the full image, followed by a half, a fourth, and an eighth, moving outward to the left and to the right.

Motifs can be grouped in rows, using them as multiple repeats as if they were quilt patches.

Arrange the images in a linear progression, all in the same orientation.

Arrange the images in a linear progression, but alternate the up-and-down direction of each motif.

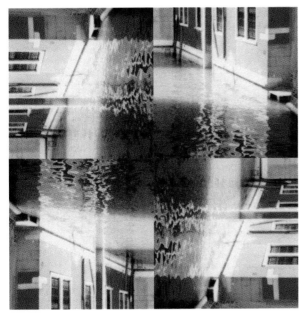

Four-Patch variations 1 (left) and 2 (right). You can also use a motif the way you might rotate patches in clockwise rotations to make Four-Patch blocks. Although these patches consist of the same visual details, they are different in their overall result. With each arrangement, a different element meets itself in the center, and different elements appear at the outer edges, creating different relationships.

Superimposing Images

Adjust your view to a rectangular format; then, superimpose and rotate a reduced-scale element within the larger image.

Superimpose a same-scale version of a portion of the larger image, and invert it.

Isolating an Area

Use your viewing window to explore the content and orientation of a square area. Then enlarge that image, and consider its potential as a full quilt—one abstract block enlarged to quilt size.

To create quilts, all of these variations would require searching for some watery, hand-dyed yardage that would simulate the fluid reflections on the water's surface.

Isolating an Asymmetrical Motif

Choose a different photograph, and isolate a square window, looking for unexpected orientations. Instead of aligning the edges of the view parallel to the edges of the photo, spin your viewer or slide it sideways and up and down to discover new elements that come into the view as you expand and move the viewer.

Facade of a pub in the Chelsea area of London

Chelsea pub detail

Following are some examples that use multiple repeats of the Chelsea pub photo detail to create clusters of patches.

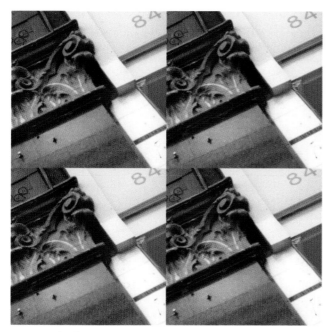

Four motifs all set in the same orientation

Four motifs spun in a counterclockwise rotation

You might find that some fragments are more engaging in linear sequences that move sideways or up and down, rather than being clustered and spun to make blocks. Four-sided asymmetrical motifs will create new secondary designs when different sides meet edge to edge.

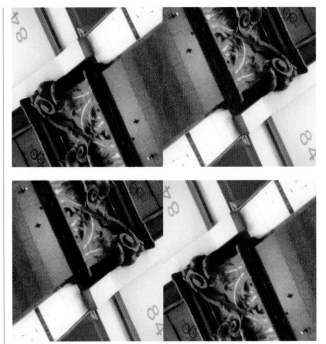

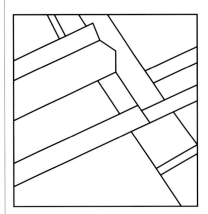

Two motifs, inverted in two variations, each of which results in different elements meeting at the center interior

Four motifs alternately inverted and arranged in a vertical row, creating a linear diagonal

A piecing diagram for the Chelsea pub detail (page 43, upper right), outlining the basic elements

Would you create the subtle color gradations in the lower left via piecing, or would you use a fabric with color gradations? Would you introduce appliqué or fusing to represent the scrollwork?

Other Options

The preceding examples focus on the use of isolated views as motifs for classically inspired clusters and blocks. Although the rotations are traditional, the results are contemporary because of the content in one photographic resource.

You can use a single photo source by returning to the full image and isolating a view that might be enlarged to full quilt dimensions. Depending on the composition of the photograph, you might use your viewer to zoom in and remove edge elements, or you might focus on an outer edge that has appealing details.

Peggy Montesano isolated a detail in a photograph of her garden. Interpreted in appliqué, it became the central motif in her pieced quilt (page 35).

Photo by Peggy Montesano

Jennifer Bigelow captured the brilliant colors reflected on a New York City building just before sunset. Her photograph blends the strong architectural forms of the actual building with the distorted lines of the reflected building.

Photo by Jennifer Bigelow

Jennifer then combined these related elements in her innovative collage *Times Square Twilight #1,* in which the elements appear as staggered multiple repetitions in varying sizes, creating an ethereal urban environment from a single source.

Gail Retka Angiulo cropped off the top edge of a photograph she took at the wharf at Killybegs, Ireland, retaining only a portion of the hull of a seagoing vessel. The result is an intriguing horizontal composition that contrasts dramatic simplicity with a textured tangle of metal chains and a flash of orange cable at the bottom edge. It could be used as the sole inspiration for an abstract memory of her trip to Ireland.

Photo by Gail Retka Angiulo

EXPERIMENTAL DESIGNING

Use copies of your photograph images to play, experiment, audition, and propose. Use your L angles to isolate views. Consider all the available sizes in your explorations—actual, reduced, and enlarged. Cut and tear. Slide fragments over and under each other. You don't have to include the same elements from the same photographs in every collage—add and remove elements as you experiment and explore. The following collages reflect innovative, rather than classic, formats.

The vivid natural colors of nearby cliffs are echoed on the buildings in Roussillon, a town in Provence, France. In this collage, Claudia Alldredge combined the details of both elements and then added slivers from photos of fall foliage in Oregon to create an impression, rather than a literal postcard view.

Inspired by the everyday environment of her back stairwell, Rebecca Rohrkaste combined angles, subtle contrasts, and shadows to invent a dramatic structure in which commonplace elements become dynamic.

In *At the Window,* Claudia Alldredge alludes to her move from Berkeley, California, to a new home in Seattle, Washington, where the change of seasons is more apparent than in California. The suggestion of a common horizon allows two seasons to be imagined as one, even when they are viewed from different windows.

Sharona Fischrup photographed a long expanse of wall covered with graffiti street art. Using a small portion of the photo, she blended a contemporary urban art form with a traditional center medallion format.

Florence Barnhart surrounded a bouquet of peony blossoms with a reflecting pool beside a city sidewalk, pairing two themes to create an intriguing combination.

In *Visions of Japan,* Emily Shuff Klainberg intermixed photographs of a shrine. She repeated them in varying sizes and composed them to invent a soaring, imagined structure in which architectural elements become vertical columns. The intricate, linear red-orange areas seem doubly complex in comparison to the larger, more massive shapes.

In Lauré Campbell's abstract collage *Boatyard #2,* receding splashes of white shapes become staggered layers of architectural details.

MAKING YOUR OWN COLLAGE

Make One Collage

Use any format you'd like to start with, choosing from classic or innovative, symmetrical or asymmetrical, and so forth. Design your collage, and secure it in place with removable tape. *Do not glue it yet.* Set it aside, or pin it up on your design wall.

Make More Collages

Try different arrangements based on different configurations. Secure them with removable tape, so you have three very distinctive collage formats.

Consider using your L-angle viewer to search for a detail within one of your collages, looking for a composition within a composition. Or make another collage using all the scraps you haven't used.

You don't need to try to project the size of the finished quilt at this point. Make the collage first, and do the math later. So far, my smallest collage for this process was 5¾˝ × 5˝, and my largest, 6¾˝ × 9˝.

Analyze Your Collages

Analyze and judge the qualities of your collages. Now is the time to be your own toughest critic. Pin up all the taped designs so you can assess them side by side. Sometimes we can convince ourselves that something is happening just because we want it to be happening. Recognize what is working and what isn't. Make visual decisions based on informed observation as well as intuitive response. And remember that these are preliminary proposals that can be modified or even scrapped.

Define and describe the compositional and visual characteristics of each collage. Answer the following questions for each proposed design:

- Does the collage have dramatic or subtle value contrasts? Are they emphatic or overpowering?

- Are the value differences so subtle that you can't see the edges of shapes? Do areas advance and recede visually, or are the values so similar that the shapes lose their definition?

- Observe the balance of the composition. If asymmetry is present, is it jarring and awkward or appealing and effective?

- Is the content harmonious or confusing?

- Is the composition classic or abstract?

Think about revisions and modifications, and make alterations as needed. The removable tape will let you make these adjustments. Evaluate. Edit. Finalize.

Finalize and Select Your Collage

Once you are happy with the design, glue down all of your final versions, removing the tape as you proceed. Mount the collages on 8½″ × 11″ white paper. Look, scrutinize, and mull. Are you attracted to one version more than the others? Why?

Find the composition that most attracts your eye, the one that most appeals to you, the one that makes you want to cancel your dinner party so you can start right now. View this one in various orientations to make sure you like it best in the position in which you designed it. I like to preserve the original collage, mounted on plain white paper, and make a copy to use as the working diagram during the enlarging phase.

Your Collage Is Your Guide

If your goal is to make a quilt that is respectful of the collage in an informal way, with more attention to its color, pattern, and value qualities than the proportions within it, you'll probably approach the enlarging phase by going directly to the design wall. Although the quilt may not reflect all the compositional relationships of the collage, you will have worked in a manner that you are comfortable with, and the results will be pleasing to you.

However, if you want your quilt to embody the visual attributes *and* the exact proportions of the collage, you need to know what those proportions are and how the pieces relate to one another before you can re-create them accurately in a larger scale. In this approach, the collage has two functions—it not only describes the content, but it also defines the physical structure of your quilt. When your goal is to make a quilt that respects the original proportions of the collage, it's better to measure than to guess.

MAKING A SEAMLINE DIAGRAM

To translate your collage to fabric, you need to make a seamline diagram. For this you'll need:

- Your collage

- Ultra-fine-point black permanent marker

- See-through ruler (Mine shows a ¹⁄₁₆˝ grid.)

- Sheet of matte acetate a little larger than your collage or a frosted acetate sheet protector/loose-leaf notebook sleeve (see Resources, page 94, for product information)

- Tape to hold the acetate in place on top of the collage

Window collage

Work from the general to the specific and from the simple to the complex. Place your collage under a sheet of matte acetate, or slip the collage into a see-through sheet protector. Use your see-through ruler and draw with the black pen on the *dull* side of the matte acetate or the frosted back of the sheet protector, outlining major shapes in the collage. Then go back into those major shapes, and draw the details you find within them. I like to use a solid line for the primary shapes and a dashed line for the secondary shapes.

The *Window* collage with a superimposed diagram drawn on the acetate overlay

As you draw on the acetate, make any adjustments and changes in the composition. The lines you draw represent the seams you will sew.

Take the time to identify any details that might complicate the construction process. Simplify, fix, and amend those places as you draw your lines. Clean up and revise vague and wobbly edges that don't seem appealing or that aren't significant to the integrity of the collage. You can also add functional seamlines that will make your quilt easier to construct.

DETERMINING THE SIZE OF YOUR QUILT

You need to have an idea of how large you want your quilt to be so you'll know how to do the enlarging. This decision may be based on whether your available fabric stash is limited to mostly medium-scale patterned fabrics that would be more appropriate in a small piece, or whether you're willing to shop for what you'll need to generate giant-scale invented yardage (which we will explore later) necessary for a larger quilt.

If the intimate size of a small piece is very appealing to you, or if you'd like to do a small experimental study first, you might designate 1″ in the collage to equal 4″ in the quilt, as I did in the pieced *Window* quilt (pages 54–55). For this size quilt, look for fabrics that reflect the collage's content, pattern, scale, textures, and personality; this will make the piece visually complex but easy to construct.

If you want to make a larger wall quilt, you can designate 1″ in the collage to equal 6″–8″ (or more) in the quilt. The greater the degree of enlargement, the more likely you will need to construct larger-scale invented yardage, because available commercial fabrics may not have the right proportions of pattern, density, and scale. You can use piecing for geometric content and traditional or fused appliqué for more unstructured shapes. A larger piece will be both visually complex *and* complex in the creation of the necessary invented yardage, but it will still be easy to join the completed sections. Refer to the chart below for some enlarging dimensions. As an example, if you are enlarging so that 1" in your collage equals 6" in your quilt, use the column under the 6" to get the various dimensions you need: 1" = 6", ⅞" = 5¼", ¾" = 4½", and so on.

Enlargement Dimensions

COLLAGE	QUILT		
1″	4″	6″	8″
⅞″	3½″	5¼″	7″
¾″	3″	4½″	6″
⅝″	2½″	3¾″	5″
½″	2″	3″	4″
⅜″	1½″	2¼″	3″
¼″	1″	1½″	2″
⅛″	½″	¾″	1″
¹⁄₁₆″	¼″	⅜″	½″

tip

When enlarging, 1″ in the collage can equal any dimension you'd like in the quilt; just remember that if you want to use Enlarging Option 2 (page 54), you'll need to maintain that ratio when figuring out how large each piece needs to be.

ENLARGING THE SEAMLINE DIAGRAM

When you're satisfied with the seamline diagram, choose the enlarging method that works best for you. What can make this a challenge is that many of your shapes will probably be irregular and may have more than four sides, all with different dimensions. But don't worry, because there are options and solutions for enlarging.

Enlarging Option 1

The quickest and most accurate enlarging method is to take your diagram to a copy shop that can make large-format reproductions. This is a good choice when your diagram includes complex pieces and unpredictable shapes, because the only measurement you'll need to know will be the dimensions of the finished quilt. For example, if the seamline diagram measures 6″ × 8″ and your scale is 1″ in the collage to 8″ in the quilt, you'll ask for a 48″ × 64″ enlargement.

Because enlargements printed directly from a drawing done on acetate can sometimes result in a murky background, I suggest transferring the drawing to plain white paper and letting the printer work from that. If your seamline diagram is on a notebook sleeve protector, all you need to do is slip a piece of plain white paper inside the sleeve.

If the copy shop paper isn't large enough to accommodate your desired size on a single surface, have them print it in sections. You can then align the sections and tape them together so that everything coincides. This will give you a scale enlargement of your quilt's layout, with everything in place and everything enlarged accurately. This blueprint can then be labeled and cut apart on the major seamlines to create templates for cutting all the elements. These templates represent finished/sewn dimensions—therefore, when you're cutting fabric, add a ¼″ seam allowance on all sides.

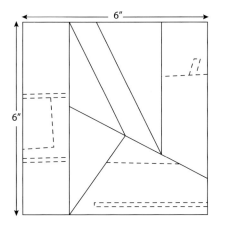

Enlarging Option 2

Many students prefer to draft the enlarged dimensions themselves by placing the acetate diagram over eight-to-the-inch graph paper that has darker lines defining the inches. With the edges of the diagram aligned with the inch lines, you'll be able to delineate the perimeter and move into the interior, projecting the enlarged sizes of the pieces. Of course, you'll still have to know what 1″ in the collage equals in the quilt so you can make the leap from a small diagram to a big quilt. A see-through

ruler will be helpful, and, yes, you'll need to deal with even ¹⁄₁₆″, because in a 48″ enlargement of a 6″ diagram, ¹⁄₁₆″ represents ½″ of cloth. Thus, if it's there in the diagram, it needs to be there in the quilt.

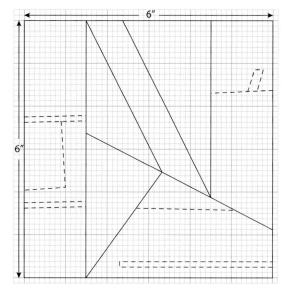

Acetate diagram layered on graph paper

Position the seamline drawing on graph paper. If your seamline diagram is drawn on a notebook sleeve protector, slip the graph paper into the sleeve. Remember, 1″ in the collage equals 8″ in the quilt. In this case, the collage is 6″ × 6″, so the quilt will be 48″ × 48″.

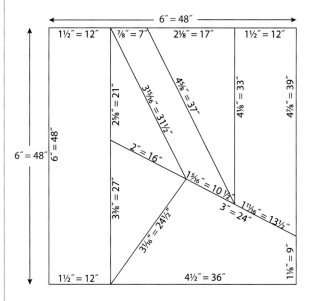

This diagram for *Window* (page 55) shows the length of each seam in the diagram, notes the reference point where one line intersects another, and projects the dimensions of every primary shape in the quilt when enlarged to 48″ × 48″.

MAKING TEMPLATES

Draft the enlargement in full size to make working templates. If your quilt will be in the 36″–48″ range, you can make the entire diagram on taped-together sheets of poster board. However, it isn't very practical to work on a paper surface that's large enough to contain all the information for a 72″-wide quilt. Instead of wrestling with an unwieldy expanse of paper that's too big to see where to make your marks and draw your lines (and that is probably too big for your table), work with clusters of adjacent shapes. You're going to cut them into individual templates anyway, and it's much simpler to draw one section at a time. Refer to your diagram as you draw the dimensions of a multipiece section. Then re-create all the interior shapes based on the information you recorded on the diagram. A 48″ ruler or yardstick might be helpful when drawing the templates.

When you have a scale-size pattern for all the templates, cut them apart and use them as you normally would, adding ¼″ seam allowances. If you have respected the measurements and proportions within the collage, your pieced and appliquéd elements will fit together in the fabric version—and that's all that really matters!

24″ × 24″ pieced study of the *Window* collage, Judi Warren Blaydon

collage+CLOTH=quilt

FINDING FABRICS

Your diagram provided a construction blueprint—now let your collage inspire the cloth and the content.

FINDING FABRICS

Once your collage is finalized and you've enlarged the scale, you'll have the *map* of your quilt. Now you can start looking for fabrics that match your vision and auditioning them on the design wall. Look on your own fabric shelves first to determine which components you already have, then you can shop for the remaining fabric. You'll find many excellent solutions not only in commercially printed fabrics but also in expressive hand-painted and hand-dyed fabrics. Without the appealing abstract essence of Mickey Lawler's Skydyes fabrics, Judy Robertson's Just Imagination fabrics, and the designs of Lonni Rossi and others, many of the quilts in this book would not be as eloquent and effective as they are.

You may want to start by gathering some preliminary fabric swatches to acquaint yourself with the unique challenges of your collage, to discover the real character of the colors, and to familiarize yourself with the process of translating paper to cloth. Search for details in your collage that may go unnoticed. For example, look for streaks of light, gradations of value, subtle changes in color, and variations in design patterns that you want to express via your fabrics. This exploratory step will help you learn to identify unsatisfying choices and quickly propose revisions. Is a particular fabric choice too murky when it's only supposed to be misty? How do the value relationships in the fabric swatches relate to those in the collage? Be your own toughest critic. Revise and resolve.

Examples of fabric swatches that might express the colors and patterns in the photo on page 13, taken aboard the *Victory* ship. Choose another England or Italy photo (pages 13–14) , and gather fabrics for it. Which elements did you see but consciously exclude? What subtleties escaped your notice on the first look?

A small area has been isolated in this photo, which was taken on Canyon Road in Santa Fe, New Mexico, and interpreted in fabrics I had in my studio. There are many more possibilities. Do you have fabrics that could accomplish those same details?

Whether your quilt will be large or small, choosing fabrics involves examining every detail of every area of the map so you'll know what to look for—and then hunting for fabrics that reflect, as nearly as possible, the same qualities and visual content. Analyze all the areas of the collage, and then gather fabrics that have visual relationships to both the major and the minor elements. You might want to supplement your stash with fabrics that reflect specific areas, or you might already have the perfect cloth but not enough of it. Depending on the size and scope of your quilt, you may be able to find ready-made, perfectly scaled fabrics that also miraculously duplicate the colors, density of the pattern, content, values, and color temperatures you need. Don't forget to look at the back of your fabrics—sometimes the reverse side is more appropriate than the front.

It's almost miraculous when you can find fabrics that are an exact color and style match *and* are proportionally appropriate so they successfully relate to the scale proposed in your diagram. You know that a pattern that looks just right when you're only seeing a 6″ × 9″ area will almost never work when you try to use it at a 24″ × 36″ size. In other words, as the scale of the piece increases, the scale of the pattern also needs to increase.

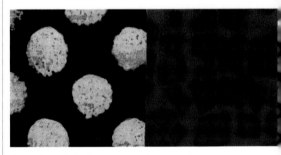

Examples of similar patterns, increased in scale

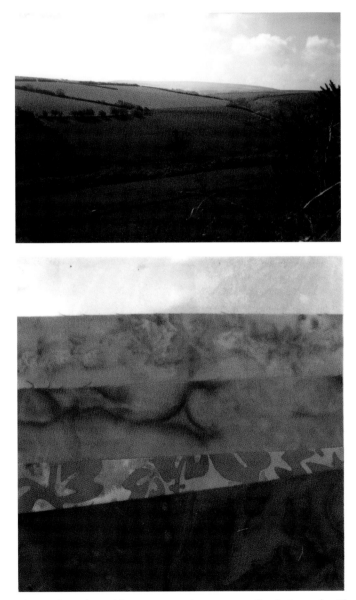

A swatch study enables you to match every area of a photograph with a proposed fabric. This collection of fabrics reflects the color content in the Lynmouth photo (also seen on page 13).

CREATING INVENTED YARDAGE

Occasionally you'll be fortunate enough to find fabrics that are suitably to scale. However, more often than not, large-scale interpretations of your collage might require that you create larger-scale yardage. In this case, you'll need to audition fabrics that can be combined to re-create the ingredients of the areas you want to enlarge.

For example, you may have a print that has exactly the right colors and values, but the pattern is too small, too widely scattered, or both. The solution is to use piecing or appliqué techniques to re-create the background, the pattern, and the density of the pattern in a way that will satisfy your need for a more expansive statement.

The scale of the pieced example is double that of the striped fabric swatch.

The desired size of the finished piece will determine whether available fabric will work or if you need to create yardage.

This small study for *Sub Rosa: Aquifer* collage (page 90) is 24″ × 24″.

At this size, only three pieces of fabric were used to articulate the landscape beneath the horizon in the center.

In the larger quilt (page 91), seventeen fabrics communicated a more complex expression of that landscape.

AUDITIONING MAJOR ELEMENTS

Pin your collage and your seamline diagram on your design wall so they don't get buried under mounds of fabric. Using your templates, audition your initial fabric choices, pinned in place per your diagram, on the design wall. Think of them as introductory recommendations that can be amended or exchanged for other possibilities later.

Analyze the details within the primary shapes, such as the sewn width of stripes and so forth. Decide how specific you want to be. Which secondary elements do you want to incorporate in your design? What would you like to revise or omit?

MAKING EDITORIAL DECISIONS

While designing and revising, don't stop until you're ready to stop. When selecting a specific collage as your map, you have made a commitment to respect the overall structure of that basic composition. Changes in the relationships and proportions of the shapes within the composition, whether inadvertent or deliberate, will alter the final result.

With the collage as the inspiration for your quilt, you might choose to adhere to the details of that composition as strictly as you can. Or you might decide, for a variety of reasons, to make changes or modifications to the visual content of certain elements once you've seen it in fabric on the design wall.

Remember that working in fabric is an *interpretation* of the collage. Photographs are photographs, and fabric is fabric—they are not the same! Sometimes what goes up on the design wall, though divergent in some aspects, is so appealing that you are willing to allow the difference to remain. Some modifications might be motivated by necessity or may simply be editorial decisions in which you deviate from the character and personality of certain visual elements within the collage, while remaining respectful to the basic structure.

You might not be thrilled at the prospect of piecing the tiny grid squares in the upper left area of the *Sub Rosa: White Square № 5* collage, no matter what the ultimate size of the quilt will be. Besides, if you squint, all those little dark squares disappear anyway, because they're so close in value! If you don't have the perfect, ready-made fabric, you could try any geometric repeat print in the right colors or just translate the values of the larger red areas. Or you could omit that detail in the piecing and introduce it in the quilting instead.

This is the 36″ × 36″ quilted version of *Sub Rosa: White Square № 5* collage. In the photo of the Wako Department Store display window (page 32), a stuffed black panther was suspended in front of hanging panels of gorgeous cloth. Although present in the photograph and in the collage, the black line of his tail is absent in the quilt because my attention was focused more on the fabrics than on the panther.

So, in spite of an emphasis on being faithful to the overall composition of your collage, a really successful interpretation does not depend on an unrelenting struggle to reproduce the infinite subtleties in every detail. The collage is simply what you started with. Do your best. The Quilt Police will not be lurking on your porch and pounding on your door if your stripes are not wide enough or if they're not there at all. And you don't ever have to show anyone your photo collage unless you want to.

I made another editorial decision in the large version of *Sub Rosa: Aquifer* (page 91). Initially, I intended to piece the rectangles and bars in the large red area above the sky in the collage. But then I realized that I didn't think I would enjoy piecing elements that would have been 1⅛″ × 1⁷⁄₁₆″ when sewn! This was an instance of something being just fine in the context of the collage, but not so great in the reality of constructing the quilt. It also occurred to me that such a high degree of precision might be out of character, as well as too much of a contrast, when seen in the presence of impressionistic hand-dyed and hand-painted fabrics. So I found a solution that worked for me—I used the red patterned fabrics in loosely arranged, pieced geometric clusters.

Do not sew together major areas and completed sections until you've seen the whole quilt proposed and on the design wall, and until after you have asked yourself the following questions:

- Are your fabrics thematically compatible?

- Do the sections enhance and complement each other?

- Do the sections enrich each other by contrast of personality? Does that strengthen or diminish the impact?

- Do your color choices reflect the colors in the collage?

- Are the interior edges of collage shapes sharp or blurred? Did you respond to that aspect?

- Does the quilt echo the value relationships in the collage?

- Were you able to introduce transparency (page 36)?

- Were you able to suggest layers as well as puzzle pieces (page 36)?

- As you moved from paper to fabric, what changes or revisions, if any, became necessary? Were those changes editorial shifts from rigid interpretation of the collage to a more free approach?

- If you made revisions, is the fabric version more compelling than the collage?

- Are there areas that don't make you smile? Why not? How can you fix them?

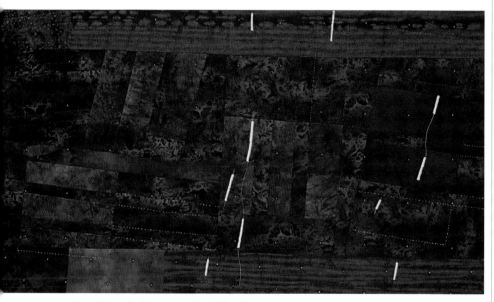

Detail from *Sub Rosa: Aquifer* (full quilt on page 91)

ASSEMBLING THE QUILT
Completing the Quilt Top

Unless you adore using your seam ripper, join all the sections of your quilt only when *you love all the parts* and *the whole* and when all the questions and issues have been resolved to your satisfaction. When you're happy with everything you see, you sew. At last!

Quilting Your Collage Quilt

Before putting the quilting foot on your machine or threading your needle for hand quilting, do some looking and reflecting.

Hang the quilt on the design wall, and clean up your workspace so the quilt is the only visual presence in the room. Leave it there for a while, and consider your options. There are no patterns for this step in the process, no rigid edicts to follow.

Now it's just you and your pencil—and your ingenuity. Make some notes. Sketch experimentally on tracing paper overlays placed over your working drawing. For example:

- Let the quilting be compatible with, and supportive of, the theme. A feather wreath superimposed over an abstract landscape is not going to earn many accolades.

- Use the quilting to define, enhance, embellish, and further express that theme.

- Use contrasting types of quilting, rather than all curved or all straight lines.

- Use different colors of quilting thread.

- Use both machine and hand quilting.

- Rather than clustering the quilting within confined areas, consider letting the pattern flow across the quilt; let it cross the line between a shape and its neighbor.

- Go back to your photographs, and look for linear content that can be quilted.

- Observe and interpret the patterns in the printed fabrics you've used in your quilt to find further inspiration for quilting designs.

Quilting detail from *Field of Dreams* (full quilt on page 22)

Let your quilting contribute both function and expression. In a practical sense, quilting stitches hold the layers of your quilt together, and that can be accomplished with utilitarian rows of parallel lines. The more important objective is to let the quilting emphasize and complement the content, character, and style of your quilt.

collage+cloth=QUILT

Favorite photos
Fractured into a collage
Blueprint for a quilt.

—*Haiku by Claudia Alldredge*

GALLERY OF COLLAGES AND QUILTS

In the same way that photograph albums are distinctively individual records that define memories of places in the world and locales we have experienced, each quiltmaker in this chapter fashioned her collage using her own unique perspective of her own unique photo resources. Some commemorated those memories through landscape or architecture; some combined natural and human-made content. Some presented nearly pictorial references, while others invented places that exist only in imagination, yet are inspired by something very tangible.

On the following pages, you'll see quilts and the collages that inspired them. You'll see evidence of enthusiastic effort and resourceful solutions. It's exciting to imagine what might happen if five people, with five different fabric collections, interpreted just one of these collages.

Sally B. Davis proposed a large composition and superimposed a viewing window over one corner to define the area she worked with. In its entirety, the collage presents an impressive urban image. By isolating one area, she found a composition within the composition. During the construction process, the bottom edge of the isolated view became the top edge of the quilt. Since most of Sally's photographs had architectural themes, the quilt feels very metropolitan and citi-fied, with architectural forms stated in fabric evoking steel and stone. The eloquent expression of foliage serves as a contrast to the abstract buildings and is created with complex detail through fusing.

Which Way Is Up? ■ Sally B. Davis ■ 47½″ × 50″

Made from commercial and hand-dyed cotton fabrics; machine pieced.

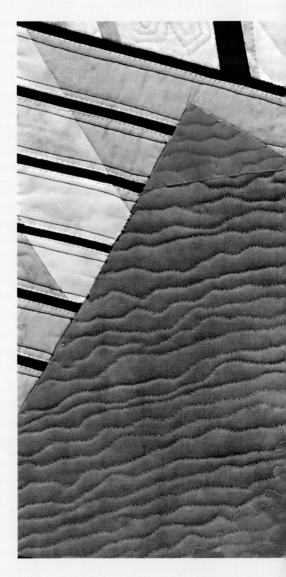

Janet Ozard Root's collage included a photograph of curved wrought iron resting on a piece of plywood onto which blue paint had been spilled. Janet found it helpful to draw the shapes to size and scale on large paper. She depicted light reflected from the iron piece and let her quilting suggest the grain of the plywood.

No Rhyme ■ Janet Ozard Root ■ 26″ × 36″

Made from hand-dyed and commercial cotton fabrics; machine pieced, fused, machine quilted.

In her second quilt, called *Astrid,* Janet combined photographs of unrelated utilitarian objects. Although the shapes reflect those in the photos, Janet executed color changes in her fabric choices. She secured the small fused elements with closely spaced parallel rows of quilting and stitched tiny circles in the area at the left, complementing the curves in the composition.

Astrid ■ Janet Ozard Root ■ 23″ × 51″

Made from hand-dyed cotton and batik fabrics; machine pieced, fused, machine quilted.

Jean Biddick's workshop experiments included collage elements from photographs of a Mexican bird of paradise plant; the spiral staircase in Madison Hall on the Morrisville, New York, State College campus; woodwork in the Winchester House in San Jose, California; a rusted metal roll-up door in Paducah, Kentucky; and an old brick wall that had been painted blue several times (page 27). In this departure from her customary compositional symmetry, she focused on the shadowed decorative bricks and used Judy Robertson's hand-dyed fabric to develop an architectural theme with her usual exemplary craftsmanship. Jean says, "For this initial foray into collage quilts, I chose to stick to the essence of the collage. If this were my eighth, ninth, or twentieth collage quilt, I might have chosen to use the initial collage as only a starting point, making different choices during the construction and quilting stages. It is all about choices."

Brickwork ■ Jean Biddick ■ 33˝ × 42˝

Made from cotton fabrics and Pentel Pastel Dye Sticks; machine pieced, machine quilted.

Photo by Toni Klopfenstein

Photo by Toni Klopfenstein

Christine Milton had her original color photographs reprinted in grayscale to introduce the challenge of expressing nature in black and white. The photos, which were taken at Christine's cottage, include the wheels and grill of her car, her garden, and the decking skirt of the cottage. Both the collage and the fabric interpretation articulate a blending of contrasting themes, a combination of the botanical with the mechanical, with foliage and blossoms seen side-by-side with steel. The impeccably crafted leaves and the hydrangeas are three-dimensional, and the silk blossoms are painted with silver. Executed after the workshop, this free-form piece, with its industrial/modern context, required an innovative display method—it was mounted with fishing line stitches sewn through tiny holes drilled in a panel of Plexiglas.

When Nature and Industry Collide ■ Christine Milton ■ 21½″ × 28″

Made from cotton, rayon, polyester, nylon, silk, metallic, and matte fabrics; paint and thread work, machine and hand appliquéd, machine quilted.

Photo by Toni Klopfenstein

Mary C. Lowe recorded memories of her former home, which was her dream house, and filled that house with remembered light. The rich, glowing colors remind her of the sun shining through a tree, glowing and casting imaginary shadows. The vertical shape of the quilt reminds us of a column or a tall tree, with patches of sunlight flickering through, and that light is expressed in a strong contrast of values and color temperatures that range from cool greens to fiery reds.

Sunny Memories ■ Mary C. Lowe ■ 31½″ × 51½″

Made from cotton, batik, and Judy Robertson's Just Imagination fabrics; machine and hand quilted.

Joanne Wietgrefe composed her collage with photos that her husband took near Beaufort, South Carolina. Sheldon Church, built in 1855, is surrounded by acres of wilderness habitat. The ruins of the church are framed by natural elements: blossoms and bark, branches and foliage, light and shadow. Joanne captured the enduring quality of historical architecture and the continuing renewal of nature in her shaped quilt. She allows us to glimpse the forest through the arched window opening.

Framed in Bark ▪ Joanne Wietgrefe ▪ 36½˝ × 41½˝

Made from batiks and hand-dyed and hand-woven fabrics; thread-work details; machine appliquéd and quilted.

Barbara Shuff Feinstein's theme was flower gardens, rock gardens, and bamboo gardens photographed in Japan. In translating the collage to fabric, Barbara chose to omit certain elements and retain others. Her value contrasts are strong, and her colors evoke foliage and blossoms contrasted with details of architecture. Barbara placed special emphasis on the leafy foliage at the upper left, not with a ponderous, hard-edged shape but with a lively edge achieved by snipping tiny feathery openings in fused fabric and then attaching it to the background so that the sky could be seen between the leaves.

Gardens of Japan ▪ Barbara Shuff Feinstein ▪ 41″ × 43½″

Made from cotton and silk fabrics; machine quilted.

The pen lines on **Carol Gilham Jones**'s collage define the seamlines of her quilt. The speared stalks of a rhubarb-like red water plant are framed on two edges by sections of a stone wall. The images are from a photo fragment generously shared with Carol by her workshop tablemate, Edy Brady. These additions provided a serene and muted contrast to Carol's more colorful photos. The scale of the stalks dwarfs that of the impenetrable stones, which are scored by subtle lines of mortar, slightly skewed. A long, green shadow silhouette frames the top of the collage, and stylized water lilies float on blue-gray water at the side edge.

Water Ways ▪ Carol Gilham Jones ▪ 26˝ × 26˝

Made from cotton fabrics; hand appliquéd, machine pieced, machine quilted.

Miriam Nathan-Roberts has been working on a series of prints using photographs taken at decommissioned military bases. Working with an extensive collection of photographs, she focused on the beauty she found in the intricate details of debris—in the colors and textures of rusty metal and concrete, in the complex saw-cut lines and checks in chunks of wood. Her quilt is like a collection of close-up views and is done in a more intimate size than is customary for her.

Mare Island Study ■ Miriam Nathan-Roberts ■ 31½″ × 35″

Made from commercial and hand-dyed cotton fabrics; machine pieced, appliquéd, and quilted.

The Spaulding Boatworks in Sausalito, California, is one of the few remaining places where wooden boats are still being built and where wooden boat–building skills are taught. Working from only three photographs, **Lauré Campbell** made five quick collages in which graphic geometric close-ups of keels and ribs of boats housed in an old wooden building became abstract and quiltlike when cut apart and reassembled. This quilt is inspired by her favorite of the five collages.

Boatyard #1 ■ Lauré Campbell ■ 36″ × 27″

Made from cotton fabrics; machine pieced, machine quilted.

Ann Rhode's collage mingles close-ups of plant life with fragments of textured bricks and posters pasted on a graffiti-covered wall. Her collage elements focus primarily on human-made materials, yet the character of the fabrics in the finished quilt expresses a more organic and natural environment. In the quilt, she modified some shapes within the larger areas of the collage and layered some fabrics over each other. The vivid slivers of red and orange provide a dazzling contrast to the muted neutrals that surround them.

Amsterdam One ■ Ann Rhode ■ 40″ × 30″

Made from Mickey Lawler's Skydyes and commercial fabrics; machine pieced, hand appliquéd, machine and hand quilted.

Light shimmering on deep water in the dark of night is just one component of **Fay Martin**'s collage that records a trip to India. In many of Fay's photographs, textures provide the major visual content. She took her inspiration from stones, weathered wood, and metal fasteners and contrasted them with imagery of water. Fay tried several collages and refinements to capture the reflections that ripple on the dark surface. She used her photo sources to create an imagined memory of a real place, showing foreground, horizon, and overhanging sky.

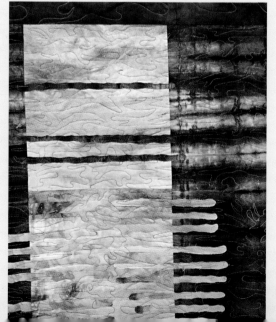

Kerala Backwaters ◼ Fay Martin ◼ 42″ × 46″

Made from cotton, hand-dyed, and commercial fabrics; pieced, machine and hand appliquéd, hand quilted.

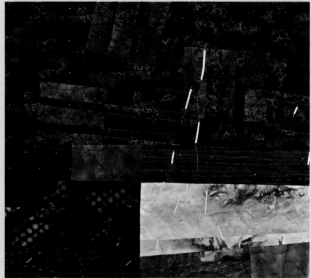

An aquifer is an underground layer of permeable rock, a fluid source for wells and springs, providing significant amounts of water. The content of this collage reflects architectural materials of walls and textural surfaces, as well as rivulets of water flowing from a fountain. The abstract landscape at the center suggests terrain and sky. A distant horizon is glimpsed through a window in the architectural structure and reappears beyond its edge. The influence of that architectural content was accomplished by using a square within a square format, in which the composition is relatively symmetrical but the value placements are not.

My collage for **Sub Rosa: Aquifer** began with the same group of nine photo sources (pages 32–33) that were used to make more classically inspired collages.

In designing the collage, I added these two photos of textured Italian walls to the collection from Japan, Mexico, and France (pages 32–33) and used elements from several of them to make this experimental collage, as well as the collage for Sub Rosa: White Square № 5 (page 60).

Sub Rosa: Aquifer ▪ Judi Warren Blaydon ▪ 54″ × 54″

Made from Mickey Lawler's Skydyes, Judy Robertson's Just Imagination, Lonni Rossi and other commercial cotton fabrics; machine pieced, hand and machine quilted.

No matter what the theme, size, or style, quilts that attract our eye do so because they embody, among others, the following attributes:

- A balance of the simple and the complex
- Recognition of the effects of symmetry and asymmetry
- Fabrics that enhance and complement one another
- The use of innovative or unorthodox approaches
- Exemplary craftsmanship

In other words, they give us something to look at and admire.

Those quilts that stay in our memory—that touch our hearts and take our breath away—reveal the eye, the hand, and the creative spirit of the individual behind the effort. They compel us to take a longer look. They speak to us, and they inspire us.

The Collage+Cloth=Quilt process allows you to work experimentally with fragments of photographic images to design a composition that exemplifies invention,

innovation, and insight. The skill, eloquence, and sensitivity with which you translate a paper composition into sewn fabrics can make a quilt that is so strong and compelling that it will stand on its own as a personal statement, with or without reference to the collage that inspired it.

The transition from the collage to the quilt is one in which all the decisions are made by you, rather than by someone else. Your quilt's success won't depend on difficult, complex, or exhausting construction methods. It *will* rely on making satisfying choices, respecting the strengths of the collage, and interpreting the composition expressively in cloth. The degree of that success is determined by an unlimited imagination and a plentiful fabric collection.

Whether your quilt reflects a traditional or innovative style, it is inspired by the content of your collage. It expresses messages that only you may understand. But although it contains personal references and obscure abstractions evoking places and events that may be significant only to you, it still entices your audience to spend more than one minute looking at it.

Although several of the compositional devices illustrated in this book evoke the traditional multiple-block repeat motifs of functional bed-size coverings (and there *is* a certain appeal to the idea of "sleeping under your memories"), I prefer displaying the final products on a wall, where their visual impact can best be appreciated.

Your subsequent use of the collage-to-cloth process may be strict or casual, and perhaps occasional. But I hope that sketching with collage elements becomes another useful design tool that will enrich your quilt-making—a design tool that is relatively rapid, that is intuitive rather than tedious, that promotes new insights, that is more original than derivative, and that allows you to approach designing in a relaxed and confident way.

If you make a collage-inspired quilt, you might approach it by following your map very specifically, to re-create the colors, patterns, textures, values, and composition of the photo fragments in your collage. Or you may respect the qualities of the collage only to the extent of being loosely inspired by its general characteristics of personality and style. In either instance, by using collages you learn to experiment with a different way of planning content and compositional ideas, and you gain experience in translating those ideas to cloth. Accomplishing these skills will guide you to new avenues and unforeseen destinations in the progress of your quiltmaking journey.

You do not have to go to Italy to find textures, to Mexico to find water fountains, or to France to find graffiti. If you are willing to slow your pace and observe the world around you, to contemplate and record the colors of a northern Michigan damselfly or the tread marks a snow tire leaves on the driveway, you will discover that there will never be enough time to make the quilts that echo the inspirations waiting in your own backyard. Just as your quiltmaking ancestors found inspiration in the world around them—in broken dishes, cobwebs, bouquets, and the structural design of a log dwelling— you can find, in your own environment and time, visual resources that attract your eye and touch your heart.

The value of your own contribution to the body of work we call Quilts is defined by your willingness to reveal what you love, to speak through your work about what you love best, and to take sole responsibility for expressing that content as eloquently as you can. Learn from that effort, and then make the next quilt. And then the next. And then the one after that!

MAKING A COLLAGE JOURNAL

One way to accomplish your quilting goals is to create your own collage journal. To get started, make L angles for a viewing window (page 30), and select your photographs. Then make two copies of each photo in actual, reduced, and enlarged sizes (for a total of six copies), keeping the originals handy in case you need more copies of a particular size. Attach one actual-size copy of each photo to the first pages of your journal or sketchbook. Use the remaining copies in various combinations to work through the collage chapter exercises (pages 34–45). Attach the finished collages to pages of the journal, recording your comments and your observations. You'll have made a beautiful visual album—a portfolio of potential quilts.

A workshop environment offers the advantage of the added learning that takes place when you're sharing the experience with other students who are also investigating the techniques and exploring the process. But whether alone in your workspace or as a student in a classroom, the process always begins by seeking and finding sources of inspiration within photographic images that symbolize and describe things you know best and love best.

It is a process in which design ideas unfold and emerge when you respond to those inspirations, when you appreciate them fully and express them fluently. They are the tangible components of a chronicle in cloth, a compelling and eloquent quilt that originates with scraps of paper and fragments of photographs—a quilt that only you can make.

THE END … or maybe the beginning.

Resources

FABRIC

Mickey Lawler's Skydyes fabrics
www.skydyes.com

Judy Robertson's Just Imagination fabrics
www.justimagination.com

Lonni Rossi fabrics
www.lonnirossi.com and at quilt shops

MATTE ACETATE

Dick Blick Matte Acetate Sheet (20″ × 25″, #55508-1001)
One side is nonglare/frosted and will accept ink.
www.dickblick.com

Graffix Matte Acetate Pad (11″ × 14″, #4354707)
www.misterart.com

SHEET PROTECTORS / LOOSE-LEAF NOTEBOOK SLEEVES

Available in clear, clear with frosted/matte surface on the back, semiclear, and nonglare from office supply stores. Matte and nonglare hold the ink well; clear is okay to use. Avery Job Ticket Holders (9″ × 12″, #75009) have a clear front and frosted matte back. Ask for them at your local office supply store.

Workshop students have suggested the following alternative options:

Office Depot Inkjet Transparency Film

3M Multipurpose Transparency Film CG6000

QUILTER'S DESIGN MIRRORS

C&T Publishing. Ask for them at your local quilt shop or order online at www.ctpub.com.